Anam Ċara & the Divine Echo

a Sermon by

Rev. "Twinkle" Marie Manning

Matrika Press
a Sermon in My Pocket Series

Thought for Contemplation:

*"The ultimate touchstone of friendship
is witness."*

- David Whyte

Dedication

For my children & grandchildren;
For my friends;
For the congregations I serve.

May you always have a sense of Belonging.
May you know you are loved
beyond measure!

ABOUT THIS BOOK SERIES

"a Sermon in My Pocket" series is
part of the "a Pocketful Book" collection
by Matrika Press.

This collection of pocket-sized books (4×6)
are ideal for poetry, meditations,
sermons or reflections, or
a collection of quotes and ideas.

This size is optimal for seasoned authors
wishing to offer a glimpse of their work
to readers in a pocket-size easy-to-carry edi-
tion. Also, this is an accessible first
endeavor for emerging authors
who desire to publish.

It is with delight we include in our
"a Sermon in My Pocket" series this
sermon by Rev. "Twinkle" Marie Manning
entitled, "Anam Ċara and The Divine Echo."

Her sermon was presented originally to the
Unitarian Universalist Church in Sangerville,
Maine, USA. It has since become one of
Rev. "Twinkle" Marie Manning's
most popular messages.

Opening Words

Today we are going to explore what it means to
Belong to one another.

There is an ancient **Ojibway Prayer**
that says:

Grandfather,
Look at our brokenness.
We know that in all creation
Only the human family
Has strayed from the Sacred Way.
We know that we are the ones
Who are divided
And we are the ones
Who must come back together
to walk the Sacred Way.

Grandfather,
Sacred One,
Teach us love, compassion, and honor
That we may heal the earth
And heal each other.

Our service today centers a mystical
aspect of belonging,
and practical ways to demonstrate
such belonging in our lives.

May all those peaceably seeking
spiritual solace feel welcomed.

Sermon: Anam Ċara & the Divine Echo

by Rev. "Twinkle" Marie Manning

Consider with me this:

There is a divine echo that whispers within every heart.

Indeed, that every soul carries with it the echo of a intrinsic intimacy.

An original echo that is brought
fourth through time
from original source.

A primal source where we
are all One.

Where love has no limit
and freedom has no barrier.

And we carry the essence of
this original echo
as a talisman of our divinity
and a reminder of the vast
belonging we are part of.

Because it is who we are.

We Belong to each other.

Consider that this divine echo,
the one I carry,
the ones you each carry,
are in constant recognition
of each other.

When we are harmonious
with each other,
the recognition alights us
with positive, light, joyful,
peaceful feelings.

Whereas, the negative, sad,
fearful or angry emotions
we feel about each other
are a result of
the echo noticing
the disharmony with Oneness.

The Celtic Spiritual Tradition
has a phrase that identifies
this sense of Oneness.

It is called Anam Ċara.
Soul Friends.

More than words, it is a concept
imbued with deep meaning.

Derived from the understanding of
the Soul as a divine echo.

Consider that each of our Souls
have a signature resonance
that radiates throughout and
around our physical bodies.

And that when we come in contact
with others,
especially our Anam Ċara,
an awakening takes place.

An awareness of the connection.

In our modern day, some
romanticize this feeling
and create limits
around its capacity.

Suggesting only one other person
on this entire planet
could be your Anam Ċara.

A soul mate.

Singular.

But the embodiment of Anam Ċara
is much more far-reaching
than that.

Anam Ċara is a blessing
we all have access to
and can share with each other.

When you have found the most
sacred place of belonging,
where your inner light recognizes
and is recognized by
those in your company,
you have found home.

hmmm :)

*When you have found the most
sacred place of belonging,*

*where your inner light recognizes
and is recognized by
those in your company,
you have found* Home.

And it is there that
Anam Ċara resides.

It is there that Anam Ċara
can be explored.

It is also there that Anam Ċara
can be challenged.

And will be.

For it is within our most
intimate relationships
that our deep bonds are formed.

And to experience intimacy,
one must be vulnerable.

And to be vulnerable in the midst
of others who are as *imperfectly
perfect* as we are,
we risk being hurt.

But we also open to being
nurtured and healed.

I ask you to consider
that while we may know things
about each other,
it does not mean
we know each other.

Yes, while we may know things
about each other,
it does not mean
we know each other.

Opening to Anam Ċara
gives us the opportunity
to know each other.

Anam Ċara.

Soul Friends.

Consider that this Divine Echo
is our touchstone;
Our reminder that
we are Anam Ċara.

And our promise that
we are blessings to each other.

My friend and colleague
Rev. Ian White Mayer
tells us that when
you bless someone,
everything in your life changes.

Some here may be
familiar with the words
of philosopher and poet
John O'Donohue
in his Friendship Blessing
where he says:

*"May you be blessed
with good friends.*

*May you learn to be
a good friend to yourself.*

*May you be able to journey
to that place in your soul
where there is great
love, warmth, feeling,
and forgiveness.*

May this change you.

*May it transfigure that which
is negative, distant, or cold in you.*

*May you be brought in
to the real passion, kinship,
and affinity of belonging.*

May you treasure your friends.

*May you be good to them
and may you be there for them.*

*May they bring you all the
blessing, challenges, truth,
and light that you need
for your journey.*

May you never be isolated.

*May you always be in
the gentle nest of belonging
with your Anam Ċara."*

Throughout time many
have spoken about
the priceless value of friendship,
and of friendship's complexities.

Unitarian forefather,
Ralph Waldo Emerson asserted:

*"I do not wish to treat
friendships daintily,
but with roughest courage.*

*When they are real,
they are not
glass threads or frost-work,
but the solidest thing we know."*

Aristotle spoke of the
highest kind of friendship
being one of virtue.

The kind of friendship
where you are
friends with someone
because of the kind of person
he or she is;
that is,
because of his or her virtues.

In Aristotle's day "virtues"
would have meant ethics.

Within the realm of our
faith traditions,
we would be speaking of our
shared values
and how we live into them.

Aristotle spoke too of the
partnership of friendships,
the idea of the virtuous friend as
"another self."

(Joined as in the echo of divinity)

Friends holding mirrors
up to one another
so they have access
to see themselves,
and each other,
more fully.

And in doing so,
improve the quality of
the people they are.

And in doing that,
enhance the quality of the
friendships they share.

Helen Schucman in relaying
A Course in Miracles
also refers to the
mirror of friendships.

She says:
*"Your (sibling) is the mirror
in which you see the image of
yourself."*

She urges us to seek to recognize
our spiritual siblings,
both as a means for salvation
and as a mechanism of blessing
and being blessed.

She affirms:
*"You will not see the light until
you offer it to your (sibling)s.
As they take it from your hands,
so will you recognize it
as your own"*

She declares that when
we meet anyone
to remember it is
a holy encounter.

*"As you see them (your sibling)
you will see yourself.
As you treat them
you will treat yourself.
As you think of them
you will think of yourself.*

*Never forget this,
for in them you will
find yourself or lose yourself."*

She continues by explaining:

*"Whenever two (Children)
of God meet they are given
another chance at salvation."*

She says:

*"Do not leave anyone without
giving salvation to (them)
and receiving it yourself.*

In other words,
your Anam Ċara
is always there with you,
in remembrance of you.

Poet and Author David Whyte
takes this theme to an even
deeper level, suggesting:

Friendship is not only
a mirror to presence
but a testament to forgiveness.

He says:

*"Friendship not only
helps us see ourselves
through another's eyes,
but can be sustained
over the years
only with someone
who has repeatedly
forgiven us for our trespasses
as we must find it in ourselves to
forgive them in turn.*

*A friend knows our difficulties
and shadows
and remains in sight,
a companion to
our vulnerabilities
more than our triumphs,
when we are under the strange
illusion we do not need them.*

*An undercurrent of real
friendship is a blessing
exactly because its elemental
form is rediscovered
again and again through
understanding and mercy.*

*All friendships of length
are based on
a continued, mutual
forgiveness.
Without tolerance and mercy
all friendships die."*

David Whyte says:
*"Friendship is a merited grace,
one that requires of us
the unrelenting commitment
of being present with
and bearing witness to
one another,
over and over."*

It is within the sacred space of this
deep dynamic of friendship
that we not only
know things about each other,
but where we really
know each other.

Ian White Mayer, whose words
I shared already in this sermon
revealing to us that when
we bless someone
everything in our life changes.

He also talks about our
deep need for
Empathetic Witness.

The kind of seeing,
and being seen,
that only happens
in the close circles
of family,
of community,
of relationships.

That's right,
in our Anam Ċara friendships.

In the Buddhist tradition,
this kind of friendship is called
the "Noble Friend."

Kalyana-mitra.

Kalyana-mitra/Noble Friends
have no pretense between them.

They witness in empathy
and in action,
with clear communication
and by gentle strength
confronting each other
with our blind spots.

Friendships at this level are
able to navigate challenges
and heal wounds
for they are willing
to negotiate beyond
the awkwardness
and uncertainties
that are paramount
when our vulnerabilities
are exposed.

It requires humility as well
to be open to
seeing through
another's experience
what we are unable
to perceive on our own.

It requires grace
to accept this sight
without defensiveness.

It requires grace
to offer this sight
without judgement.

To be present with each other
in this way
is a testament of trust
and the embodiment
of faith.

And faith is certainly needed
when we shine
the gentle light of the Soul
on our wounds.

We are indeed
a wounded gift to each other,
but a beloved gift nonetheless.

David Whyte speaks about
the benefit of this
depth of friendship
in saying:

*"The ultimate touchstone of
friendship is witness,
the privilege of having
been seen by someone
and the equal privilege
of being granted the sight
of the essence of another,
to have walked with them
and to have believed in them,
and, sometimes
just to have accompanied them
on a journey impossible
to accomplish alone."*

For some believe it is
the hard times that
make us stronger,
yet I believe
it is the good
we are wrapped up in
while facing hard times
that help us
carry our broken pieces:

The love of our family,
our friends,
our community,
these are what make us stronger,
keep us whole,
keep us moving forward.

This good is the
beloved community
we all seek to belong to.

As a faith community,
how do we become accessible
to facilitating the nurturing
of that kind of friendships?

Author Anne Lamott
has some advice for us
where we could see ourselves
as a Lighthouse.

She points out that:

*"Lighthouses don't go
running all over an island
looking for boats to save;
they just stand there,
shining!"*

Every day that this congregation
opens its doors
(*in-person AND online*),
it stands as a lighthouse,
shining,
beckoning those
who would be saved from
the heartaches of the world
into our loving embrace.

Beckoning our Siblings,
our Anam Ċara,
Home.

Anne Lamott, in her book
*Small Victories:
Spotting Improbable
Moments of Grace,*
has a chapter containing her essay
about "The Book of Welcome."

Her essay could well be the outline
for a liturgical Midrash
that attempts to fill in
the spaces left blank
in the Hebrew Scriptures.

In "The Book of Welcome,"
Anne imagines a Bible book
that was never written.
Or if it was written,
it has been misfiled and lost.

She speaks of scriptures that
would provide
a set of guidances
and assurances and principles
that would create
a sense of security and belonging
for Earth's residents.

She writes:

*"The welcome book
would have taught us that
power and signs of status
can't save us,
that welcome
— both offering and receiving —
is our source of safety.*

*Various chapters and verses
of this book would remind us
that we are wanted
and even occasionally
delighted in,
despite the unfortunate
truth that we are
greedy-grabby, self-referential,
indulgent, overly judgmental,
and often hysterical."*

In her version, we would be
accepted for our gifts
and our apparent flaws.

We are welcome because we
Belong to each other.

Anne asserts that
Somehow that book
"went missing"...

*Perhaps "when the editorial
board of bishops pored over
the canonical lists from
Jerusalem and Alexandria,
they arbitrarily nixed
the book that states
unequivocally
that you are wanted,
even rejoiced in."*

She says
"We have to write
that book ourselves."

And I say,
we have to write
that book together.

And we do write
that book together
with every encounter
of Welcome we share.

We write The Book of Welcome
every time we acknowledge
the echo of divinity
in our hearts
and in our Anam Ċara.

We write The Book of Welcome
every time we gather
together in response
to our members' needs,
hopes and dreams.

We write The Book of Welcome
every time we answer
the call to invite and greet
new ones into our spiritual family.

We write The Book of Welcome
every time we unite
in the name of this congregation
and our Faith traditions
and evangelize in response
to the calls of
unity,
and justice
and being on the side of love.

We write The Book of Welcome
together every time
we open the doors
to this congregation
and invite in
those peaceably seeking
spiritual sanctuary.

A Blessing for
this Congregation

*May this house of worship
be blessed.*

*May this congregation
be loving to each other.*

*May your doors remain open
to welcome the stranger
seeking spiritual solace
and inspiration.*

*May you deepen your friendships
in trust and in faith.*

*May you find peace
and create peaceableness
as you live into our shared values.*

May you be joy-full
and thoughtful;

May you be
a light of grace
and a beacon of welcome
to the world;

and

May you remember that we
Belong to each other.

Amen.

Closing Words

May we each recognize the
Echo of Divinity in our hearts.

May we recognize the
Echo of Divinity in each other.

May we recognize our
Anam Ċara when we meet them.

May we love them
every day of our lives.

And so it is.

Blessed Be.

Discussing Anam Ċara
and The Divine Echo

Key Words and Phrases:
The Divine Echo
Anam Ċara
Soul Mates
Holy Friends
Mirror
Blessing
Lighthouse
Welcome
Belonging

Talking Points:
1.(a) How does the concept of The Divine Echo resonate with you? **(b)** Have you felt this sensation or sense of deep connection? If so, discuss.

2.(a) How do you feel about the concept of Anam Ċara? **(b)** How does it differ from (or is it similar to) your understandings of Soul Mates or Soul Friends?

3.(a) What does it mean to Belong?
(b) When, where and with whom have you felt the deepest sense of Belonging?
(c) How have you struggled with Belonging?

4. Discuss the Holy Friendships you've experienced, especially when you (or they) have been faced with challenging circumstances. Include how you may have been mirrors for each other. As well as how being witness to circumstances was beneficial.

5. The Ojibway Prayer suggests that it is up to us to heal our brokenness. What are some examples of how we can do so?

6. How does your congregation practice radical welcome to **(a)** members,
(b) new-comers.

7. Discuss ways your congregation can serve as a Lighthouse in your wider community.

Rev. Dr. "Twinkle" Marie Manning, D.D. is an ordained interfaith minister, retreat leader, poet and liturgist. She received her Doctor of Divinity, D.D. through the University of Sedona and is a member of the International Metaphysical Ministry. Twinkle strives to include many philosophies in her service. Her ministry often focuses on the earth-centered, esoteric, spiritually connected, community building and social justice aspects of her faith.

One of her ministry's core teachings is that of
Living Life As A Prayer.

Twinkle is a multi-disciplinary artist. She a published author and poet, intuitive acrylic and watercolor painter, mystical sketch-artist utilizing pencil, ink and charcoal, with additional creations spanning video, audio and digital media.

She is an award-winning television producer and podcast host. She is a former radio talk show host, columnist and luxury lifestyle magazine editor. She is an experienced public speaker, retreat leader and interfaith minister.

While most her published work is inspirational non-fiction and poetry, Twinkle has recently published her first children's book and is about to publish her first young adult and contemporary adult trade fiction novels.

Her poetry and writings have been included in spiritual rituals, funerals, memorials, wedding ceremonies, blessingways, and coming-of-age gatherings in many locations around the world.

Common themes of her ministry and writings include:

Building The Beloved Community,

Curating Peace on Earth,

Embodying Compassion

Creating Spiritual Practices
that Honor the Earth and the Human Experience

For more information about Twinkle, visit:
www.TwinklesPlace.org

Matrika Press is an independent publishing house dedicated to publishing works in alignment with transformational religious and spiritual values and principles. Its fiscal sponsor is UU Women and Religion (www.uuwr.org) and Melusine's Haven (www.MelusinesHaven.org).

Matrika derives its name from the 50 letters of the Sanskrit alphabet called "the mothers" aka "Matrika." Kali Ma used the letters to form words, and from the words formed all things...as with the Bible: *"in the beginning was the Word."*

People of all backgrounds and faiths agree:
Words are powerful.
More than that: *Their vibrations are creative forces;*
they bring all things into being.

Matrika Press is part of the ministry of Rev. "Twinkle" Marie Manning and part of the larger nonprofit church known as Twinkle's Place, also known as RSOTDE. Matrika Press, along with TV for Your Soul, serve as the creative branch of the ministry's media projects. Matrika Press publishes anthologies, memoirs, poetry, prayer and ritual manuscripts, and other books to bring transformation to the world.

www.MatrikaPress.com

FIND OUT HOW
YOUR CONGREGATION OR GROUP *CAN HOST*
a local UU Talks in your community. UU Talks is a
speakers series, similar to TED Talks, where Speakers
will speak about topics aligned with UU Values.
Join Us!
www.UUTalks.org

*Above pictured: Inaugural UU Talks event
at the UUA Boston, 2017
Peter Bowden, Matt Meyer, Lydia Edwards, Rev. Allison Palm,
Jim Tull, Anna Huckabee Tull, Regie Gibson, Marlon Carey,
Rev. Hank Pierce, Rev. "Twinkle" Marie Manning*

OTHER TITLES BY THIS AUTHOR

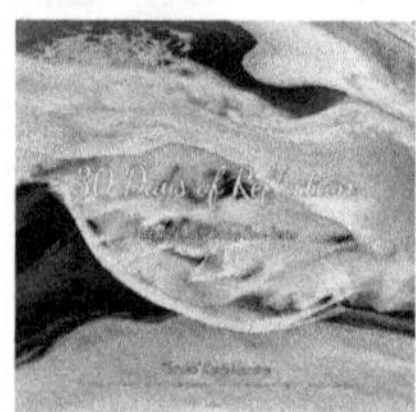

www.MatrikaPress.com

Cardinal Magic is the first book in the **Mora Mulberry** series about a little girl who lives by the ocean on a farm in Maine with her mother. Mora and her friends are so happy to share their adventures and lessons with you! This book is about kindness and welcoming new friends. It also offers strategies to help overcome stress.

www.MoraMulberry.com

GODDESS GUARDIAN
ORACLE CARDS

Designed by: "Twinkle" Marie Manning

Published by
MATRIKA PRESS

www.TwinklesPlace.org/GoddessCards

Empowering
W O M E N
Salon Gatherings
&
Signature Events

"Twinkle" Marie Manning
is the founder of the
Empowering Women TV project.
She and her friends host these amazing
gatherings! If you would like to attend,
or Host one,
in your community, visit:

www.EmpoweringWomenTV.org

Twinkle's Place

RETREAT CENTER & ARTIST RESIDENCY
www.TwinklesPlace.org

www.365DaysOfPoetry.com

Anam Ċara and The Divine Echo

a Sermon in My Pocket Series
by Matrika Press

This sermon by **Rev. "Twinkle" Marie Manning**
centers a mystical aspect of belonging.
It is an exploration about interconnectedness,
deep friendship, radical welcome
and what it means to belong to one another.